THE SACRED BLOOM

THE SACRED BLOOM

A GRACEFUL UNFOLDING OF HEALING AND WHOLENESS

KHIN LAY MAW

Cover design by: © Khin Lay Maw, 2025
Cover illustrations by: © Khin Lay Maw, 2025
Interior illustrations by: © Khin Lay Maw, 2025
Text by: © Khin Lay Maw, 2025

Publisher: Khinspirations Creative Designs LLC
For permissions or inquiries, contact: khinspirationsauthor@gmail.com

First Edition
Paperback ISBN: 979-8-9993297-4-5
Ebook ISBN: 979-8-9993297-2-1
Hardcover ISBN: 979-8-9993297-7-6
Printed in the United States of America

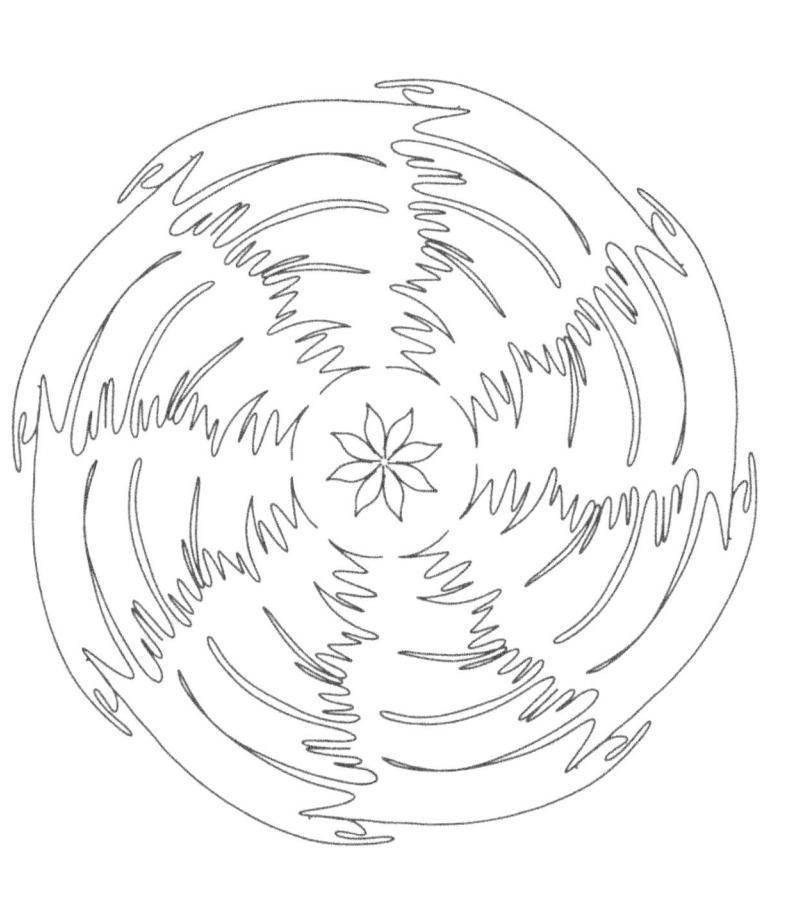

DEDICATED TO YOU!

It is my belief that we are all somehow interconnected in this vast, beautiful world.

If I can sprinkle a little magic dust on your journey, helping you heal and bloom into your best self, then I would consider my life's goal, and this book's purpose, fulfilled.

It is my heartfelt hope that reading this collection of poems is a healing experience for you; that it allows you to embrace life to its fullest potential and discover your authentic purpose. I wish you nothing but a life bursting with joy and conviction.

Here's to unraveling your true path—that's my ultimate mission!

ACKNOWLEDGMENTS

First and foremost, I would like to thank God for granting me knowledge through my life experiences and guiding me on my journey. I was meant to live this life and go through different life experiences so that I could create and pass down a beautiful legacy that will last forever to the next generation. I am forever grateful to God.

I would also like to thank my family, which has served as a beautiful support system, offering guidance, encouragement, and love. My parents, my husband, and my child have all been unwavering pillars of support throughout my life. I am deeply in love with these souls. I also wish to extend my gratitude to my beautiful sisters, nieces and brothers-in-law. They hold a permanent place in my heart.

To the relatives, friends, teachers, and mentors whose influence has been instrumental in shaping my journey, I extend my heartfelt appreciation.

Finally, my special thanks to all my readers. You are the heart of this book. Thank you!

It was through the collective contributions of everyone in my life and in this world that I have come to embrace the beauty that surrounds me. Thank you for allowing me to express my deepest gratitude!

FOREWORD

For as long as I can remember, poetry has been a natural part of me. The words seem to arrive effortlessly, flowing through me with a quiet ease. Writing poems feels like something I was simply meant to do—an instinctive way to express what lives in my heart.

I believe this ease is the product of my connection to my emotions and feelings which give birth to words that resonate with life. When we allow ourselves to truly feel our emotions, the language of the soul begins to speak. That's why poetry feels so soothing to me. It invites me into a gentle state of flow, where I'm no longer resisting my thoughts or emotions, but simply moving with them.

In the moments when I write or read a poem, I am completely present. Much like painting a canvas, the process of writing poetry draws me in so deeply that time and space fade away. I become immersed in the beauty of expression, in the quiet joy of creating something meaningful.

Poetry helps me reflect the beauty of this world and the depth of the life experience.

CONTENTS

PART I: INTRODUCTION 1
 WHAT IS A POEM? 3

PART II: SEEDING – CHILDHOOD 5
 MY MOTHER 7
 MOTHER'S LOVE 9
 PURE BEING 11
 MY FATHER 13
 SWEET CHILDHOOD 15
 TREASURES OF LIFE 17

PART III: GERMINATION – LOVE AND HEARTBREAK 19
 FIRST LOVE 21
 CLAPPING WITH ONE HAND 23
 CHAINED 25
 LOVE OR PAIN 27
 CONFUSION 28
 CLUELESS 31
 QUESTIONING 33
 LITTLE BY LITTLE 35
 UNFULFILLED 37
 TRUSTED 39
 HOPEFUL 41
 MEND IT 43
 WILTED 45
 CROSSING OF THE BRIDGE 47
 BUSY POET 49
 IN MY THOUGHTS 51
 MY LOVE SONNET 53
 I KNOW A GIRL 54

PART IV: GROWTH – LIFE 57
 SUCCESS 59
 BE RESPONSIBLE 61
 JUST BE 63
 KEY TO SUCCESS 65
 FANCY CLOTHES 67

DECIDE   69
TODAY I FAILED   70
LESS IS MORE   72
UNKNOWN YET EXISTING   74

PART V: FLOWERS – MOTHERHOOD   77
EXPECTING   79
BUD TO BLOOM   81
NEW TO THE WORLD IN THE PANDEMIC   83
THE POWER OF THE UNSEEN   85
UNSTOPPABLE   87
LIVE A LITTLE   89
AN EXQUISITE SOUL   91

PART VI: STORMS – ILLNESS   93
FALLEN HAIR   95
CONSUMED   97
THE OTHER SIDE   98
UNDERSTOOD   100
INTERCONNECTED   103

PART VII: POLLINATION – HEALING   105
SPRING IS HERE   107
MEDITATION   108
GIVE   111
HEART OF GOLD   113
LIBERATED   115
SLIPPING   117
CHOOSE   119
SELF LOVE   121
HEALING   123
MIND   125
EMPTY YET FULL   127
HEALED   129

AFTERWORD   130

ABOUT THE AUTHOR   133

PART I:
INTRODUCTION

WHAT IS A POEM?

poems need to rhyme
poems need to have stanzas
poems need to be spelled correctly
poems need to have correct grammar

all that poets want to do is
pour their hearts out

can't a poem simply touch a soul?
can't a poem simply inspire?
can't a poem simply uplift a weary heart?
can't a poem simply soothe a restless mind?

my humble aspiration is
nothing more than
to evoke your healing through
the tender embrace
of my inspiring verses

what is your take on a poem?

PART II:
SEEDING –
CHILDHOOD

MY MOTHER

when my mother says
I will be fine,
I am fine

when my mother says
I will succeed,
I succeed

when my mother says
I will achieve,
I achieve

mothers have powers,
mysterious powers,
to heal the human soul

their blessings have energy
pure energy

I am healed
when the process I allow

MOTHER'S LOVE

a mother's love is
unmeasurable

a mother's love is
full of sacrifices

a mother's love is
unbelievable

a mother's love is
soul-soothing

a mother's love is
a mother's love

healing, beautiful, and
unconditional

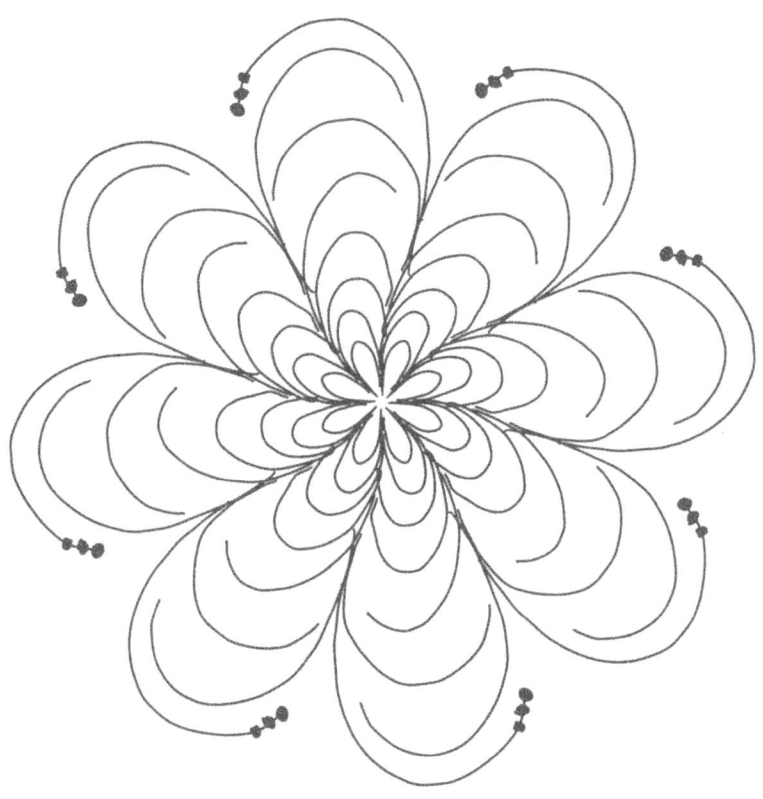

PURE BEING

Mother,
when I grow up,
will I be loving like you?

Mother,
when I grow up,
will I be kind like you?

Mother,
when I grow up,
will I be beautiful like you?

Mother,
when I grow up,
will I be soothing like you?

Mother,
when I grow up,
will I be enduring like you?

Mother,
when I grow up,
I want to be divine and pure
just like you

MY FATHER

the first man on earth
that I fell in love with

the first man on earth
whose hands I held

the first man on earth
who taught me about life

the first man on earth
who allowed me to soar

the first man on earth
who endured everything for my sake

the first man on earth
whom I thank dearly for his life

the first man on earth
whom I will forever remember
my father, my hero

SWEET CHILDHOOD

a sweet treat conjures
moments of childhood
that can never be lived again

the fragrance of a flower
the melody of a piano

the dance of bubbles
the joy of licking a popsicle

the high of running in the park
the vibes of dancing to a song

the excitement of sliding down
the slow sway of a swing
the kiss of the wind on the face

everything was purely magical
bursting with vibrant energy

seek it again
and you will find that
this energy has been in you
all along

TREASURES OF LIFE

the pretend pot I cooked with
the marble I played with
the doll's hair that I combed
the china plate that I broke

the book that I tore
the biscuit box I opened
the cake rusk I dipped in my milk
the cabinet that was too tall to reach

the friend who annoyed me
the teddy I hugged daily
the buddy I sat with
the ants that I became friends with

little treasures of life
will always be remembered

PART III:
GERMINATION – LOVE AND HEARTBREAK

FIRST LOVE

it was just an ordinary day
when love came into my life

pierced my heart at first sight

and left without giving anything away
received without being reached for

CLAPPING WITH ONE HAND

a true, deep love
had fully captivated me

the love was so powerful
it became more mesmerizing
than the lover himself

I am captured by this pure love

now it is just me
and my love

one sided,
but two of us

CHAINED

love—a word said so easily
yet impossible to understand

some react to it so dreamily
some get lost in its command

a word so strong
it pierces deeply through the heart

the feeling lasts lifelong
it sets everything apart

I cannot describe it
nor can I deny its existence

it brings to the hearts tranquility
yet at times creates flaming resistance

love—a word that cannot be explained

until we breathe our last,
it is destined to keep us chained

LOVE OR PAIN

love is a subject often praised,
while pain remains unvoiced

suffering in silence, unseen,
the anguish is kept inside

love dances in joy,
but its hidden pains
I must now bravely face

even with this newfound knowledge,
my love endures each challenging phase

now, the question remains unchanged:
in this epic battle, who truly reigns,
love or pain?

CONFUSION

I want to start this poem
but I do not know how
perhaps I'll begin simply
with what I feel right now

if I tell you the truth,
you will be amazed,
there's not much to hide,
and few questions to be raised

life is simple
and it keeps on going
you fall in love
with or without knowing

but there will come a season
when you are confused,
you whisper the love words
that went so long unused

although you know how you feel,
the feelings you must conceal

worry less about how life should go
just go with the flow,
like an aimless firefly
let just your shining love glow

I want to end this poem
but I don't know how

perhaps I'll end it simply
with a heartfelt, tender vow,

I shall give you love as infinite as sea
my love, I'll always wait for you
under a falling-hearts tree

CLUELESS

your smiles
your gazes

your words
your concern

if it was all empty
why did I feel so full?

your lies
your sorrows

your eyes
your farewells

if it was all shallow
why was so I deeply immersed?

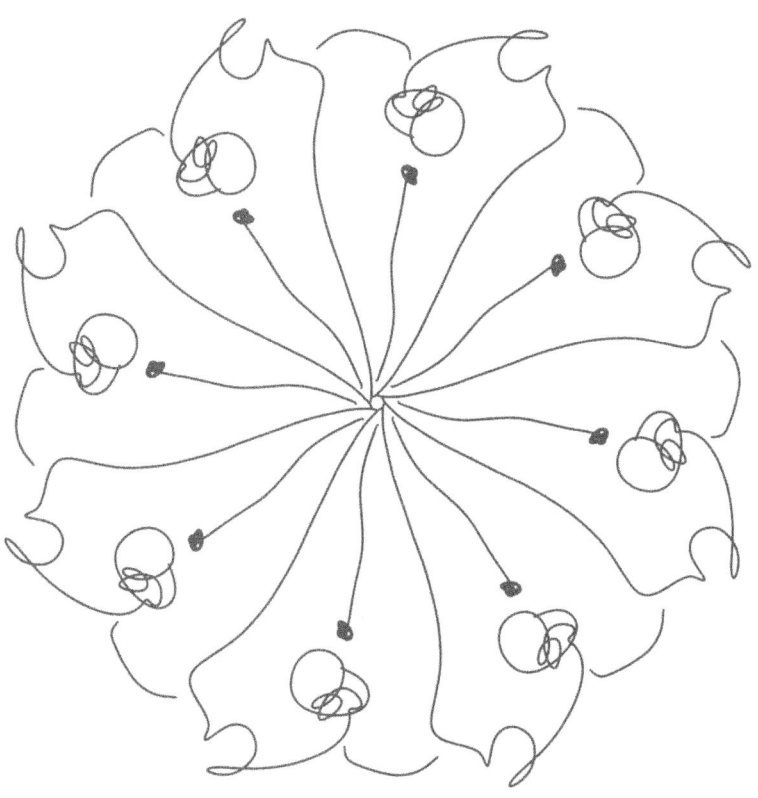

QUESTIONING

my heart questions your unfaithfulness.
are you the lover? am I the skeptic?

my pain questions your cruelty.
are you the lover? am I too fragile?

my tears question your heartlessness.
are you the lover? am I insecure?

my days question my loneliness.
are you the lover? am I truly unloved?

my love questions your love.
are you the lover? am I the beloved?

my doubts aside, you are my love,
and yet, I still question myself.
am I the hopelessly devoted lover?

LITTLE BY LITTLE

when I fell in love
it was little by little

I did not know you were acting
I learned it little by little

everyone said it was a game
I felt it little by little

the ignorance started to hurt me
I embraced it little by little

I was the only hand clapping
I understood it little by little

when I fell out of love
it was little by little

UNFULFILLED

promises left unfulfilled
feeling extremely strange
wanting something unsure
writing something unknown

days passed by
some memories getting held back
wanting to be completely forgotten
yet some memories are rising up
to find the happiness that
may be impossible now

TRUSTED

broken once
then lost forever

taken once
and gone forever

cannot be little
cannot be too much

just a clear yes or no
that is trust

HOPEFUL

when you suffer a betrayal,
rebuilding trust can be challenging,
but the world
is vast and diverse

give it a few chances

who knows what treasures
you will discover

MEND IT

when a cloth is torn,
repair it

when a heart is broken,
mend it

gather your hopes and dreams
stitch up the shattered heart with seams

it is your heart
you let it fall in the first place
now it is time to reassemble it
with grace

WILTED

well my love,
my life is similar to that of a rose

it is always looking towards the sun
waiting for the perfect bee

it is attractive
and alluring

without its family of leaves
it will not be perfect

it has a hard time
with its pricking thorns

it's thrown away
when it's wilted

always searching
for someone
who will water it
full of love

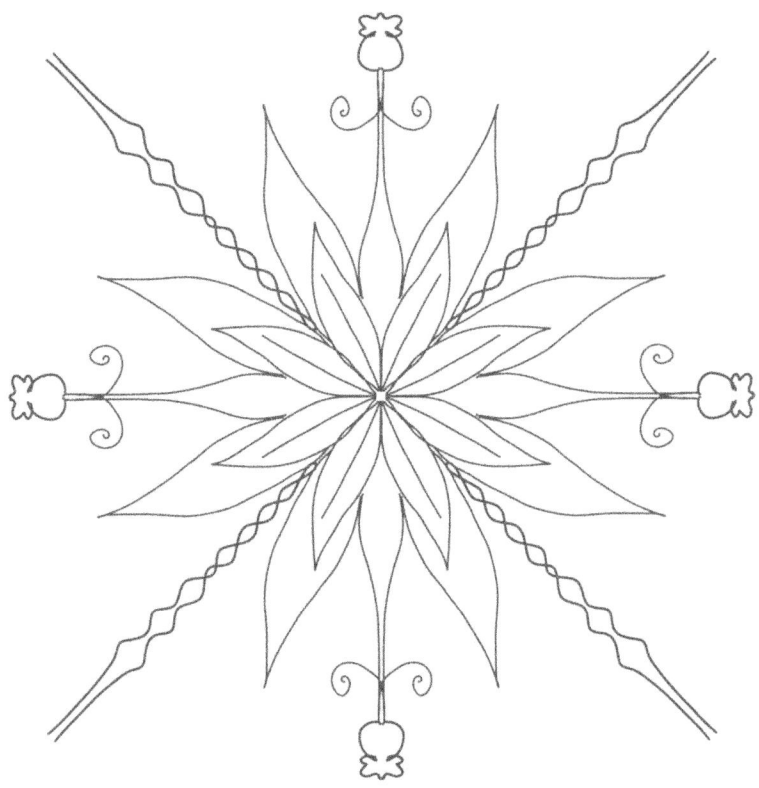

CROSSING OF THE BRIDGE

finding something true
wanting something faithful
writing something secret
meaning something totally different
days go on...

tears are held back
memories are gone with the breeze
diary entries are ended with sadness
thoughts are locked up in the soul
words are left unsaid and unheard
days go on...

questions arise
hearts beat again
flowers bloom
birds look for soulmates
eyes look for love
dreams evoke certain things
yet...words go unexpressed
and days go on...

yet days go on...
and words...
go unexpressed...

BUSY POET

when you fall in first love
you transform into a rhapsodic poet

when you fall out of first love
you turn into a brooding poet

when you find the right love
you become an preoccupied poet

no time to spare for poetry
all your time is in blooming love

IN MY THOUGHTS

you reside in my thoughts
you reside in my heart

if I were to lose you
I could not bear what I would lose

no matter how our paths diverge,
love remains in our hearts

and so, we unite
to love each other forever

our love is renewed
all I can think of now is you

MY LOVE SONNET

with so much love I have written
my perfect sonnet; indeed

with feelings that my heart kept hidden
I have formed a poem
you have always wanted to read

your heart is innocent and pure
your love is warm and giving

my beautiful heart that you tried to cure
with your love started living

there's so much to say about you
yet I kept scratching my head,
so much we have been through
but I will remember each moment instead

a companion and a partner
given from above

please let me live in your heart
will you, my love?

I KNOW A GIRL

I know a girl whose eyes were red
with tears from a broken heart
she said love would not get out of her head
so she tried to exorcise it with art

I know a girl who kept dreaming
and hoping love would come
for love, she kept screaming
yet the love she received was none

I know a girl who once gave up on hope
wishing for all other stories to be complete
her life was a downhill slope
but she kept her wishes sweet

I know a girl who is so naive
her cleansed heart makes her simple
her love taught her to believe
she looks up to the stars that twinkle

I know a girl who found love so true
he said her heart is so pure
he made her sky oh so blue
that her wounded feelings found a cure

I know a girl whose dreams were fulfilled
if you ever doubt your love and hope
your wishes should not be spilled
know that love is a beautiful, pure envelope

I know a girl who kept her dreams alive
in love, she strongly believed
it taught her heart to survive—
hers is the story of the sacred bloom
you have just received

PART IV:
GROWTH – LIFE

SUCCESS

do not chase success
define your own

if you are happy,
you are successful

are you happy?
are you successful?

BE RESPONSIBLE

they say we must save the planet
and paper is made of trees

so I use the fog
on my glass shower door daily
to plan my life

JUST BE

be yourself
and never get lost

or change to fit the norm
and never find yourself again

KEY TO SUCCESS

the key to success
is consistency

the key to failure
is wavering

some of us learned this
the hard way
through wasted years
that we can never get back

be consistent

FANCY CLOTHES

the day I wore
a nice watch
fancy clothes
a matching purse
high heels
everyone opened doors for me
everyone greeted me

the day I wore jeans and old shirt
and did not dress up
my existence was not recognized

why are clothes so important?
more important than me?
I am here
do you see me?

DECIDE

we split our world into two
half inside our devices
half outside our devices

even though we are here
we are not here
even though we are there
we are not there

inside the devices
everything seems to be happening
yet nothing is happening

outside the devices
nothing seems to be happening
yet everything is happening

where is the most happening in life?

TODAY I FAILED

today I failed
I get up and try again

today I failed
I get up and try again

today I failed
I get up and try again

today I failed
I get up and try again

today I failed
I get up and try again

today I failed
I get up and try again

today I failed
I get up and try again

how long should I keep doing this?

until it changes to
today I succeeded
I got up and flew

each failure drew a step of the ladder
to your higher self
do not get held up on the first rung

LESS IS MORE

when there is light
every room is lit
people spread around
find their comfort spaces

when light goes out
everybody gathers
just in one tiny room
and lights one candle together

when there is water
each house is its own oasis
sovereign

when there is drought
one bucket is all that we have
bringing us together

when we have less
we value more

when we have less
we share more

good values are taught
while we have less
so less is truly more

UNKNOWN YET EXISTING

last night, I looked up to the sky
one question came to my mind: "why?"

I could not figure out to whom I belong
no matter what they said,
I kept myself strong

each day passed by with few facts known
whom do I call mine?
who is my own?

life is like a ballet dance.
unless you're steady on your toes
you do not stand a chance

when I stop writing,
listen, still, to my heart
I find I've lost a line or two
let's go back to the start

last night, I looked up to the sky
one question came to my mind: "why?"

a poem without inspiration
has nevertheless gained admiration
a poem with an ending uncertain
for the meaning is vague and insane

yet it indeed was a poem
and that you cannot deny
my hand stopped writing
as my heart said goodbye

one question came to my mind
as I looked up to the sky
last night was when I asked,
"my dear God, oh why?"

PART V:
FLOWERS –
MOTHERHOOD

EXPECTING

is it a boy or girl?
what does it matter? it's our child

will the child be smart or slow?
what does it matter? it's our child

will the child look like mom or dad?
what does it matter? it's our child

do you want a boy or girl?
what does it matter? it's our child

the child will be loved.
love is the only thing that matters
it's our child
a beautiful child
just the way every child is

BUD TO BLOOM

the news of your arrival
blossoms in her heart
with the focus your survival
her life sets off to a new start

she carries you with gentle care
and shields you from harm
tough and rough, her life she bears
with just thoughts of your charm

as she waits daily for you to come
she yearns and counts each day
she looks at her belly, round as a plum
with more love than she can say

days turn to nights and nights to days
as she prepares for your arrival
her love glows with the warmth of sun rays
she cares not for herself, only your survival

a mother is the most blessed soul
she carries the world in her womb
her children make her heart whole
beloved buds that bloom

NEW TO THE WORLD IN THE PANDEMIC

loud noises in a cozy sac
eating fluid in the dark pitched black

I walked every lane
I felt every pain

nine months of togetherness
immeasurable love and tenderness

the world welcomed me with open arms
I arrived with all my might and charms

not knowing the hardships ongoing
I touched some lives and set them glowing

innocent, this world I entered
immense and unconditional love, I surrendered

I pray that the world finds its cure
I am new to this world
my devotion is pure

THE POWER OF THE UNSEEN

the power of an unseen enemy
a thief of lives and serenity
I wonder how much grief one heart can contain
every day more are left deeply in pain

spreading like wildfire with full force
no one knows when it will end its course

hoping that we get through this soon
all of us have to dance to its tune

let's keep our hopes way up high
with so much at stake, we look up to the sky

let's unite and pray together
as we fight this deadly weather

united, we are stronger than the beast
strategize when it's expecting us the least

in tough times, stay calm and sane
do not let the world's efforts go in vain

UNSTOPPABLE

I am a bud that will slowly bloom
do not count my failures
I would fail, they assumed

"You cannot do it," was what I was told
with harsh and painful words
all my hopes you sold

I put together my shattered dreams
woke up with a refreshed mind

I am unstoppable
little did they know

I would, fail they assumed
do not count my failures
I am a bud that will slowly bloom

LIVE A LITTLE

sometimes you forget to breathe a little
because your priority is not yourself

sometimes you forget to take a little
because you are so used to giving

sometimes you forget to smile a little
because your soul is left undernourished

sometimes you forget to cry a little
because your child needs the most comfort

in the life of a mother
in the midst of your sacrifices
remember
to live a little

AN EXQUISITE SOUL

the most innocent eyes
the softest lips
the puffiest cheeks
the cutest nose
the darkest hair

the beautiful manners
the most loving hugs
the kindest thoughtfulness
the gentlest understanding
the soothing care

the sharpest intelligence
the purest handsomeness
the most considerate gestures
the most unconditional love

this soul has been carefully
hand-crafted by God

I am astonished by
the beauty of my child

PART VI:
STORMS – ILLNESS

FALLEN HAIR

once there were many
then they started to fall

for all kinds of reasons
I cannot recall

illness, aging, just like that
I once looked like a doll

so temporary this life is
and this journey

with grace, I'll embrace the fall
I must remember
I will always be a doll

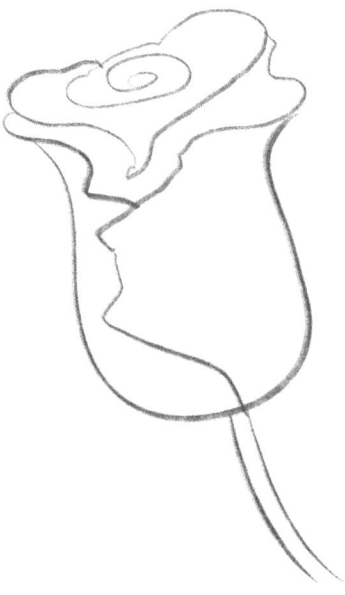

CONSUMED

while I drink my tea
I look out the window to see

withering is the tree
devastated the bee

the planet is not for free
a good reminder for you and me

THE OTHER SIDE

there is a painting
there is a bench
there is a curtain
there is a clock
there is no one sometimes
there is someone sometimes
there is quietness outside
there is noise deep inside

as I look out the window
I see people doing their routines
I see cars going their ways
I see buildings standing firm
I see a wall that separates me and all that happens
I see the clock ticking one second at a time
I see my feet trembling with the desire
to get out of this place

today I pass by that same hospital room
while doing my routine
traveling in my car
along the same highway
only this time I am on the other side
and time is running like a horse
my heart filled with gratitude
that I am no longer in that room
but my prayers go to the person
who is now looking out that same window
I pray that they can come
to this other side soon

UNDERSTOOD

your experiences are so unique
that when you go through an event
everyone says they can understand you
but can they truly understand?

each event in your life is so profound
experienced by you and you alone

even when you experience the same things as others,
the way you experience them is
your very own

so how can anyone truly understand
your story?
your journey?
your battles?
your struggles?

how can anyone truly step into your shoes
to know what you went through?

how is it that we can sympathize with others
and comfort others,
but we always have to bring in our own stories?

that's because we only truly understand
what we went through
but to make people feel better
we feel that we have to bring in our own stories
as comparisons
we had to tell people that what we went through
was much more, so they feel better about what they've
gone through
we were trying to help them
by making a comparison

but how can it be that
someone truly understand another's struggle?

INTERCONNECTED

you are you
I am me
yet why does our pain feel the same?

you are you
I am me
yet why does our yearning feel the same?

you are you
I am me
yet why does our suffering feel the same?

you are you
I am me
yet why does our unconditional love feel the same?

are you?
am I?
in this vast universe,
are we not interconnected?

PART VII:
POLLINATION –
HEALING

SPRING IS HERE

the sun rises
the leaves are renewed
flowers bloom
little bees fly by

the breeze kisses my face
the tire swing sways
the air is fresh
spring is here

your soul is touched
embrace it all
it is a homecoming

MEDITATION

please, Mind, keep quiet
Mind runs its race

please, Mind, keep quiet
Mind catches a flying bug

please, Mind, keep quiet
Mind travels across the world

please, Mind, keep quiet
Mind recalls yesterday's meal

please, Mind, keep quiet
Mind stops a minute
just to think more

please, Mind, keep quiet
Sshhh. Sshhh. Sshhh

alright, Mind, tell me
what are you thinking?

tell me more
yes, more and more

let these thoughts flow
I am a willing spectator

Mind goes quiet
says no more

thoughtless
truly free

meditating
me and my mind

GIVE

happiness from taking is
short-lived

happiness from giving is
permanent

so give
just give

HEART OF GOLD

I do not have a heart of gold
I see a homeless man
on street being cold ♪

I do not have a heart of gold
I see orphans
needing hands to hold

I do not have a heart of gold
I see the poor
and the hopes that they've sold

I do not have a heart of gold
I see the elderly
with hopes and sadness they withhold

I do not have a heart of gold
I see patients suffering
their hands oh so cold

I do not have a heart of gold
I see many stories that are left untold

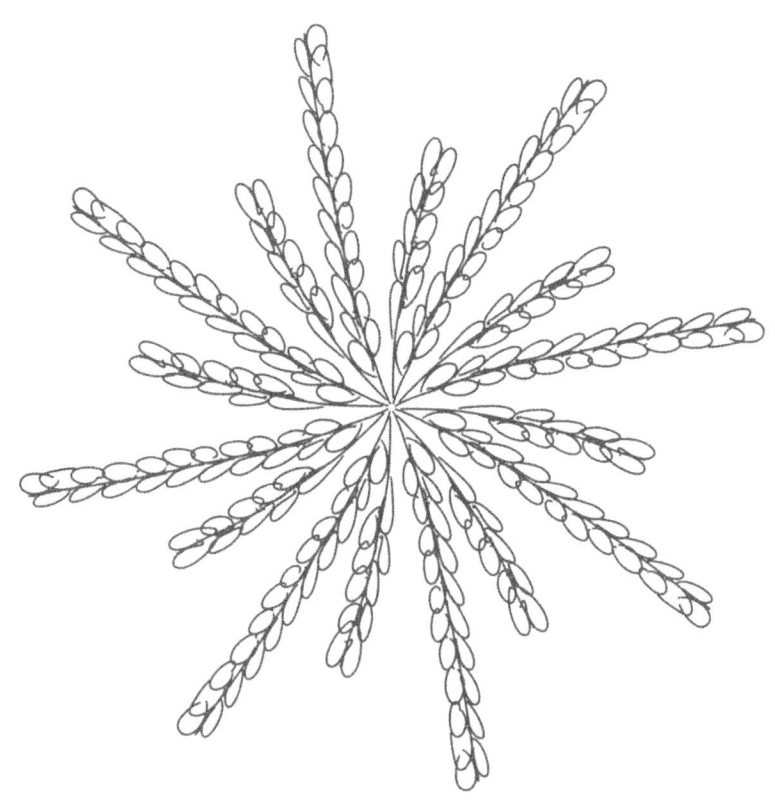

LIBERATED

today when I woke up
I had to write

words were flowing
from my head
like a river
freeing itself
to be a waterfall

so I let them flow
to let them go

SLIPPING

time does not heal anyone
time is not a therapist

time does not stop for anyone
time is not an automobile

time does not love anyone
time is not a person

time just exists
time moves on its own

if you waste time,
time will waste you

if you respect time,
time will respect you

before it slips away
catch time
the right time

CHOOSE

is it simpler to live the life you love?
is it cleverer to love the life you live?

both take time to achieve
you have to decide for yourself

you are capable

SELF LOVE

when the sun rises
and your eyes open
you are the first person
in your world
to wake up
to know that you exist
to experience your existence

self-love means just that
you are the first person
to receive your kindness
your love
your care
your presence

the rest will fall into place

HEALING

when you are emotionally hurt
when you are upset
when you are looking for
someone to heal you
visit the vastness of your inner world

the power of healing
cannot be found in time
nor in another person
nor anywhere else

it is in your hands
it is in your mind

you decide
how long to take to heal
one minute
one hour
one year
one lifetime

it is in your hands
it is in your mind

MIND

mind is like a young child,
who wants to explore
who wants to test their limits
who wants all the attention

to tame the mind
you have to be calm
embrace your breath
allow it to flow

after all
it is like your child
if you accept it with love
and nurture it
with the purest thoughts

it will flourish
it will bring
rays of sunshine
to your life

EMPTY YET FULL

when I quiet my thoughts
I hear my soul

my soul is blank
my soul is empty
my soul is silent
my soul is timeless
my soul is vast
my soul is alone

in this emptiness
I found me

I am whole
I am heard
I am beautiful
I am loved
I am soothed
I am healed

HEALED

healing is a journey

healing takes love
healing takes kindness
healing takes comfort

you are soothing
you are kind
you are loving

fill your luggage with
love,
compassion,
kindness,
forgiveness,
awareness,
travel on this journey
to heal yourself

you can heal
you will heal
you are healed

you have bloomed!

AFTERWORD

The heart and soul behind this poetry book is the desire to offer a sense of comfort and possibility and to remind the reader that transformation is always within reach, no matter where someone is in their journey. If even one person finds solace, strength, or inspiration in these words, then this book has served its purpose.

Life brings us countless lessons, and in each life experience, there is an opportunity to uncover our inner strength and resilience. I have always seen failures as steps being built in the staircases that ultimately lead to success. When we begin to see challenges as stepping stones rather than obstacles, the journey becomes a little gentler and more bearable.

Though difficult times can feel long, painful, and uncertain, it's important to remember that within you is the quiet power to grow, to heal, and to become stronger.

I am sharing this poetry with a sincere hope that it touches your heart, uplifts your soul, and helps you move through life with greater ease, strength, and joy.

The Sacred Bloom brings the power of imagination to life, encouraging the reader to compare their life to the life of a sacred flower as it grows. Starting out from a small seed, rising through the mud and overcoming harsh environmental factors, blooming petal by petal, it flourished. The beauty of this process is similar to our human life experiences. With each new experience in life, we grow a little stronger and become more resilient. We bloom to become the best version of ourselves. Such is the beauty of life, and as you move through your life experiences, I hope that you can look back and are able to see yourself blooming petal by petal and becoming a higher, better version of your true self.

ABOUT THE AUTHOR

Khin Lay Maw is an artist and author who has a deep passion for finding meaning in life's experiences. Through poems inspired by the lessons she's gathered on her journey, she hopes to offer gentle inspiration to others—encouraging transformation, healing, and a deeper connection to oneself.

Khin is a devoted wife and loving mother who resides in the United States, where her heart is rooted in family, creativity, and compassion. Her writing is a soft invitation to find kindness in everyday moments, and to help nurture a more loving and mindful world.

In the quiet spaces of her life, Khin finds joy in painting, meditation, learning new things, exploring nature, and capturing its beauty through photography.

🌐 www.khinspirations.com
📷 instagram.com/khinspirations
f facebook.com/khinspirations
@ threads.com/khinspirations
◤ substack.com/@khinspirations
▶ youtube.com/@khinspirations

www.ingramcontent.com/pod-product-compliance
Lightning Source LLC
Chambersburg PA
CBHW060612130626
46555CB00002B/502